LITERARY MAGAZINE
BEHIND THE SCENES OF READING AND WRITING

FOUNDED BY DIANA NIXON
USA TODAY & INTERNATIONAL BESTSELLING AUTHOR

LITERARY MAGAZINE

Issue: SPRING 2021
Founded by: Diana Nixon

Senior reviewers: Aura Matei, Carine Verbeke

PR Manager: Samantha Soccorso

Cover design by: Amina Black

"Step into a scene and let it drip from your fingertips."

_M.J. Bush

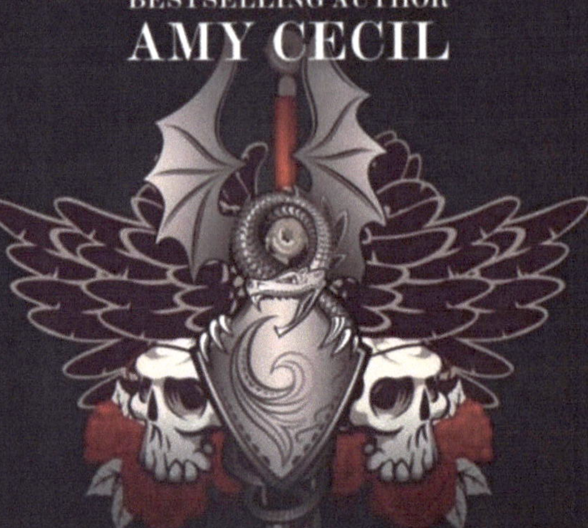

COVER STORY

AMY CECIL PRESENTS

Knights of Silence MC
& The Enemy Duet

Amy Cecil is an award-winning and best-selling Indie author of both historical and contemporary romance. Her penchant for Austen fan fiction, won her the title of Favorite Historical Romance Author (2016-2017) while her MC series has won several awards throughout the indie community. Recently, she has expanded her repertoire to the thriller and erotic genres.

For as long as she can remember, Amy always had a book (or two) that she was reading for the love of getting lost within its pages. Amy has been heard to have said, "I've never given much thought to becoming a writer myself until I realized that if I hadn't written my own version of Mr. Darcy, I might have run out of material to read."

And thus, her first novel was born, A Royal Disposition. In the words of Miss Austen herself, "I wish as well as everybody else to be perfectly happy; but, like everybody else, it must be in my own way." Ms. Cecil writes to do just that.

She lives in North Carolina with her husband, Kevin, and their four dogs. When she isn't creating her next masterpiece, or traveling the country for book signings, she enjoys spending time with her husband, friends, and of course her fur babies.

"Face life as you find it-defiantly and unafraid." -Nietzsche

I&S: Welcome back to Inks & Scratches, Amy! It's a pleasure to have you with us again. This time we are going to talk about your Knights of Silence MC series. Tell us a few words about the series in general.

The Knights of Silence MC series is a five-book series with an added duet spin-off, titled The Enemy Duet. The series focuses mainly on one biker club and their president, Ice. During the series the club is forced to combat a rival club and silence an evil twin, travel to Ireland to help one of their brothers, serve as mafia muscle and deal with the loss of a brother and the fallout resulting from his death. You would think that would be more than enough, but then, although these guys are tough bikers, they love, and they love hard. So many of them are dealing with relationships of love, friendship and even loss.

The Duet series intertwines within the five books of the Knights series and they really need to be read in order.

I&S: In one sentence make our readers want to buy the series.

You can't go wrong with the Knights of Silence MC/Enemy Duet because each page is loaded with hot, alpha bikers and the strong women who love them along with steamy biker and mafia drama, that will leave readers gasping!

I&S: Who is your favorite character from the series and why?

It's funny that you ask that. When the series started with the first book, Caden, aka Ice was my favorite character. He is the star of the series. The entire series begins and end with him and his childhood sweetheart. But when I got to the last book, Sainte, it all changed. While I will always love Ice and he will always hold a special place in my heart, I have to say that Nick "Sainte" Saintero is now my favorite character. He's the kind of character that you love to hate. He's smart-ass and annoying, but loyal to the core. He says what he thinks, and the consequences be damned. He is no saint as his name implies. He's consuming and infuriating all at the same time. He's a sexy badass and will stop at nothing to get what he wants. After all, what else could you expect from a retired mafia hitman.

I&S: The Enemy Duet is a spinoff of the series. What shall we expect from it?

While the Knights are based in Pennsylvania, the Vitali family rules over New York. The Enemy Duet will take the reader, along with Knights into the world of organized crime, Italian style. The duet is full of drama, including a cartel, a kidnapping and a rat within the family organization. The main characters, Michael Vitali and Zaira Bonito experience a love that transcends time, although it takes them a while to realize it. The MC has close ties with the Vitali family, and we are first introduced to Sainte in this series. There is an additional novella that will be published soon that serves as a prequel to the Enemy Duet, titled Fatal Enemy. This story was featured in the Voyages of the Heart: Venice Anthology.

I&S: Rumors are, there will be two more stories added to the series. What are they about?

Is it still considered a rumor if it's true? Yes, one of the stories has been published in the Voyages of the Heart: Dublin Anthology, but will be a standalone novella and a prequel to the Knights Series, titled Ace of Hearts.

The second book will also be a standalone, but part of the series. It revolves around one of the series' most beloved character, offering a look into his life and how he became the character everyone loves. Unfortunately, that is about all I can say about this one because I don't want to give away any spoilers for those who have not read the series yet. But I can tell you that you can look for that release in late 2021.

In the next year or so I also plan to publish a "next generation" to the Knights series as well.

I&S: Where did you get ideas for the stories from the Knight of Silence MC series?

As many of my readers know, I started out writing Jane Austen Fanfic, primarily Pride and Prejudice variations. While writing my second release, I kept thinking that Darcy and Elizabeth's story be great in a modern-day scenario with bikers. And honestly, that's how the series started. It was going to be a Pride and Prejudice variation. When I got halfway through writing the book, I realized I just couldn't make it work. The more I made Fitzwilliam Darcy talk biker lingo, the more I would cringe. But, by that time, I was so invested in the whole biker world that I just said screw it and made it its own story. And well the rest is, as they say, history. For those who have read the series, you will notice a few similarities to P&P that I just couldn't give up.

TEASER TIME
Sainte: Knights of Silence MC, Book 5

I woke the next morning and found Honey gone. I expected as much. Did she really think she could play me? I knew what she was up to all along. I wasn't born yesterday, and by playing along with her, I got laid. Win-win in my book. I'm kinda mad at myself for not playing along longer, but now, she knows I'm onto her. Still lying in bed, I can't help but laugh at the expression on her face when I asked her if she was leaving or staying. It was priceless. I have to say, it was a smooth move on my part. Not to mention she was a good fuck. Indeed she was, and

I am sure there will be plenty more where that came from. I'm sure in time I'll be her new addiction. Once she starts, she won't be able to stop. Yeah, I'm a cocky SOB.

Other than showing her where I stood, one other thing came from last night's escapades: Honey didn't snort any coke while she was with me. It's probably the longest she has gone since she started back.

I know I can't cure her, but I can make sure she gets the help she needs. She also has to openly admit she has a problem and want help before any healing can happen. From what I've been told, she's been through this before. I understand it was before she came to the MC, but she still knows the drill. And once she figures out that Ice isn't gonna put up with her shenanigans, she'll see she has only two options: get clean or get out.

I get out of bed, pleased with myself, and get in the shower. Fifteen minutes later, I'm dressed and heading downstairs. I'm surprised to find Honey sitting at the bar with her cup of coffee. She got up early this morning. Yeah, probably because she wasn't so fucked up last night. But still, progress.

"Good morning, Feisty Pants," I say as I pass her and head into the kitchen. She doesn't say anything back, but I hear her grumble a bit.

I get my coffee and head back toward the bar. "Somebody woke up on the wrong side of the bed this morning."

She glares at me. "Nope, just the wrong bed."

"Yeah, keep telling yourself that, sweetheart." I laugh, and it seems to piss her off more. She's looking pretty ragged, which I take as a good sign. She still hasn't taken a hit since yesterday. Maybe she does have this under control now that she knows someone is watching her. It's a good thought, but I doubt it.

I take a sip of my coffee. "So, darlin', what's on the agenda for today?" She looks up at me, and I wink at her. "Will you just go away!"

I nudge her shoulder. "Oh come on, Feisty Pants, admit it. You enjoyed every minute of our little tryst last night."

I can just see the irritation on her face, and frankly, I'm loving it. "I did not!" she snaps. Her reply causes me to laugh out loud. "Oh, guess those moans meant you hated it. Damn,

Honey, I totally misread you." I wait for a response, and when she just ignores me, I lean in close. "Or maybe it was you screamin' 'Fuck me, Sainte.' I'm not sure, darlin'. Maybe you can refresh my memory," I say teasingly. Nothing pleases me more than to get her goat and, better yet, getting her to the point where she has no comeback.

"You're an asshole, Sainte." She grabs her coffee and leaves, heading upstairs to her room.

Naomi Springthorp

Naomi Springthorp is a born and raised California Girl. She lives in sunny San Diego with her feline fur babies and believes everything in life has a soundtrack. Baseball fanatic is an understatement, she spends half of each year cheering for her team–the baseball pants are a bonus. Naomi writes baseball romance, romantic comedies, 90s throwback, and contemporary romance—usually featuring music, a hot hunk, some heat—and sometimes a little sweet.

An All About the Diamond Romance is her baseball series, which actually features baseball not just a player. The details of the game are on point and her stories portray living with the baseball lifestyle. The stories have banter and unintentional humor, as well as characters with quirks.

Muffin Man is a reader favorite that will make you laugh in the first 5 pages. Who would argue with a hot romcom about a fireman and a super sassy heroine who only does one-night stands? Hot and funny. Fire Captain Muffin is your perfect date and won't let you down.

Betting on Love takes you back to the 90s and Vegas! Full of heat, angst, chemistry, and music, without the technology we all have in our everyday lives. No cell phones. No social media. Nobody is reporting on your every move. The trouble you could get into and not get caught. Meet the hot, sexy, tattooed, shaggy-haired metalhead that goes commando in his 501s and the woman who falls for him on a girls night in Vegas.

Falling for Prince

1-Click your copy now and share with your friends! It's a standalone, short romantic comedy that's part of my baseball romance series. Are you ready to meet our hot 3rd baseman, KC Prince?

Coming soon...

The Bed – Romantic Comedy
The Panty Thief – Romantic Comedy
Going Down – Romantic Comedy
Up to Bat – Baseball Romance
Stalking Second – Baseball Romance
Confessions of an Online Junkie – Epic 90s Throwback
...and more

Love & Devotion

A DYNAMIC DUO OF
TONYA CLARK & NAOMI SPRINGTHORP

I&S: *There are so many things that Love & Devotion combines. How did you come up with the idea of this duo?*

We met each other at a signing and instantly created a friendship. We manage to keep each other grounded when it comes to running Love & Devotion and we work great together when it comes to shooting what we call now our Love & Devotion models. It helps that there are lots of times we are on the same page when it comes to ideas, and we are both ready to jump with both feet in when it comes to our events making them fun and bigger and better.

I&S: *Tell our readers more about the book signing events that you organize.*

Love & Devotion features primarily indie authors, all from varying romance subgenres. Our models join us for the event and are available to sign photos and books. We have a VIP Lunch with the authors and models that is included with our VIP ticket, as well as an hour of early access. We end our event with raffles for gift baskets of books and related items, AND our shirts off the models backs event. You can join our Facebook Group at facebook.com/groups/lovedevotionevents for video of our shirts off the models backs drawings and photos from the event.

We are expanding our next event to include a party on Friday night and a party on Saturday night, both hosted by a model and sponsored by authors! We can't wait! In fact the Friday night party is the Unbirthday Party--an Alice in Wonderland themed Tea Party--and all attendees are invited to dress the part. We have been working on putting our costumes together. The Saturday night party is the Storybook Pub Party and it will be hosted by Kole O'Shea himself!

I&S: As a publisher, what do you think makes a book a bestseller?

I believe it's a lot of timing. So far, we have earned Amazon Hot New Release, but we are still working on achieving bestseller. At this time, we have only published our anthologies, but hope to work more with individual authors as we get more under our belt.

I&S: Anthologies are one of the things that you work on. We would like to know more about the Young Crush anthology.

Young Crush is our newest anthology that has been released this March. It's all about those first time crushes, the first kiss, maybe even a little heartbreak. Our team of authors for this anthology did an amazing job bringing YA and NA together. It's a compilation of never before published stories by DC Renee, Danielle Wright, Rayne Elizabeth, Naomi Springthorp, Victoria J. Hyla, Jillian Liota, Rachel Lyn Adams, Stefany Rattles, Tonya Clark, and the debut of Raelyn D'Coursey.

I&S: What author services do you provide and how can authors book them?

We are growing this part of the business slowly, so far we offer cover photos, custom photo shoots, head shots, formatting, newsletter service, editing referrals, and some graphics services. Linktr.ee/lovedevotion or email lovedevotionevents@gmail.com for details.

I&S: What in your opinion is the hardest part of being a publisher?

We are open to giving everyone a chance and some require more guidance than others. The hardest part is working with authors from different backgrounds and varying levels of experience. We love working with new authors and guiding them through the process. We want to put out a quality product and if we can help an author polish their story, it's all worth it.

I&S: What are your favorite promo tools that you think most effectively help authors spread the news about their books?

We use social media. I'm a big fan of BookBub and love that they have different options to get your books in front of people that read. We share all over Facebook. We also take advantage of online email services to promote our releases.

I&S: How long does it take to organize a book signing event? What problems do you face during the organizing process?

We have managed to pull a signing together in six months, but it's enough work to take as long as a year. The larger events that we are looking into hosting take a little more energy. Problems we face in the past year have been COVID and having to reschedule. However, when we aren't booking around a pandemic I think it's just getting the word out to the readers.

I&S: Share one of your favorite memories from the events that you participated in.

The expressions on everyone's faces when the models shirts came off was priceless! The excitement of the winners--readers and authors both--was unanticipated.

Personally, having an attending author walk up to my table and buy my books because they loved them made my month! But, nothing compared to having a fun and successful signing with my partner in crime.

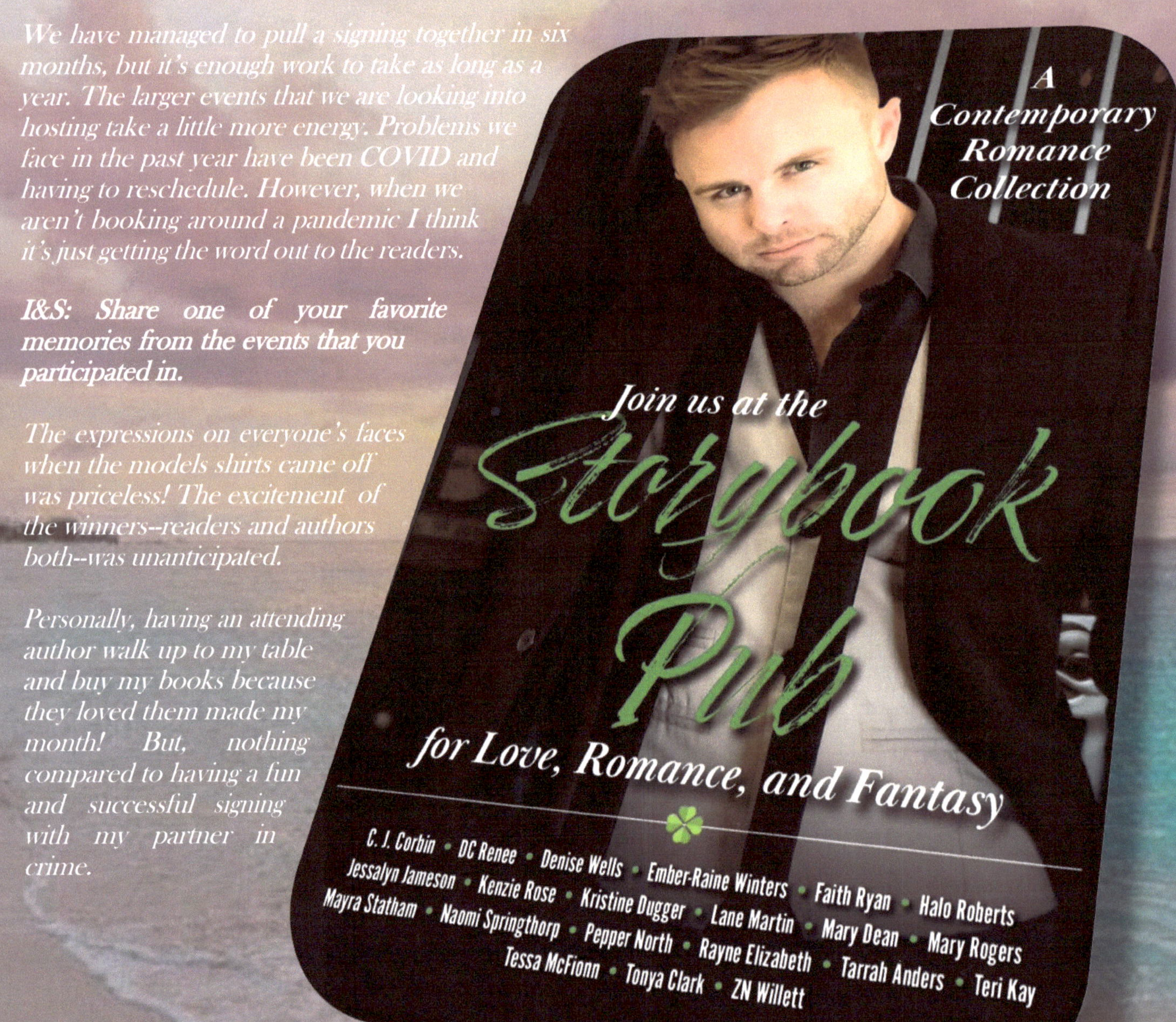

Storybook Pub
Christmas Wishes
Denise Wells • P.T. Macias • Naomi Springthorp • Ember-Raine Winters
Alexi Ferreira • Rachel Radner • Jenn D. Young • Claire Davon • Mary Dean &
Stephanie Nichole • E.K. Woodcock • Aviva Vaughn • Tonya Clark • C. J. Corbin
Rayne Elizabeth • Melody Dawn • Teri Kay • Kenzie Rose

Tonya Clark

Tonya Clark lives in California with her hot firefighter hubby and two amazing daughters. She is a little over obsessed with the color purple and wishes she could wear a hoodie every day of the year. Not only does she write about hot guys for readers to fall in love with, she also has the amazing job of photographing those hot male and female models for the covers.

Add in some very little spare time for the multiple soccer teams she coaches.

She writes contemporary romance, but likes to mix the sub genres up with a little suspense, sport, second chance, MC and shifters, and deaf romance.

ALL ABOARD!
ROMANTIC ADVENTURE AWAITS!

Some men go into the military wishing they were immortal.

Not Wyatt Sutton. He hates being immortal. Especially at first. The constant daily pain, the gear, and the worry of his brothers and family but when Glen comes to him with an idea for their future, Wyatt can't help but agree.

Wyatt becoming the president of the Midnight Defenders, he soon realizes that his wife and unborn child are in the crossfire of everything that comes the club's way.

TEASER

"Tell me what?" he asked again. This time his voice was harsher.

I sighed. There was no way around this. No way to push it any farther back, and definitely no way to come up with a quick lie.

I set the mug down onto the table and placed my hand back on my stomach and stared at him right in the eyes. His beautiful hazel eyes stared back at me.

"I...uh. Well actually we..." my voice shook. My mouth was dry, and I was having trouble coming up with the best way to tell him.

Damn it! Why did this have to be so hard? Why couldn't I get excited like a normal human? Why did I have to worry about how this will affect the club? Or how the hell this was even happening in the first place.

Renee Shearer

*I&S: Welcome to Inks & Scratches, Renee!
First of all, tell our readers a few words about yourself and the origins of your writing career.*

Thank you very much! I'm 37 and I'm from a small rural town in Michigan, and I've been a published author for 3 years.

I have always written short stories and poems but it wasn't until I had characters talking to me for almost a year before I started writing my first novel.

I&S: What genres do you prefer working in and why?

I love writing in the paranormal romance genre in the sub-category of Reverse Harem. This is my favorite category because I love the creativity with the magic and unknown. And I write Reverse Harem's because who doesn't dream about having a group of guys treat you like a queen?

I&S: Tell us more about your latest story and its characters.

My latest story is going to be released in early May, and it is a spin-off of a side character from my first series. Jess was the babysitter in Cursed by Fate, now she is battling her own demons with her guys by her side.

I&S: What are you currently working on?

Twisted Souls is the first book in Jess's story. She is a soul catcher, there is only ever 1 until a new person is marked for it. They are tasked with the job of hunting down evil so vile even hell doesn't want them. With the help of her soul swords, she traps them in an alternate universe so they can never harm anyone again. She is on the hunt for a Prince of Hell and his vampire lover when her past comes back to haunt her. Her ex-lover-- Demi-God-- Dakota, is determined to get her back, no matter the cost.

I&S: What promo tools do you use to promote your stories?

The only promo tools I use really are Facebook and Tiktok (@renee_shearer_rhauthor) for social media. I'm really big on TikTok, I find a lot of research material and followers from it. Otherwise, I just run my mouth about them all the time and get a lot of word-of-mouth sales (smiles).

I&S: What is your favorite part of being a story creator?

I love knowing that when people read one of my books, they can escape for a little while, like I was able to when I was younger.

I&S: What in your opinion is the most challenging thing about writing books?

The hardest part to me, is when my characters, or invisible friends as my husband calls them, stop talking to me. That and editing, I will deep clean my house to avoid edits (smiles).

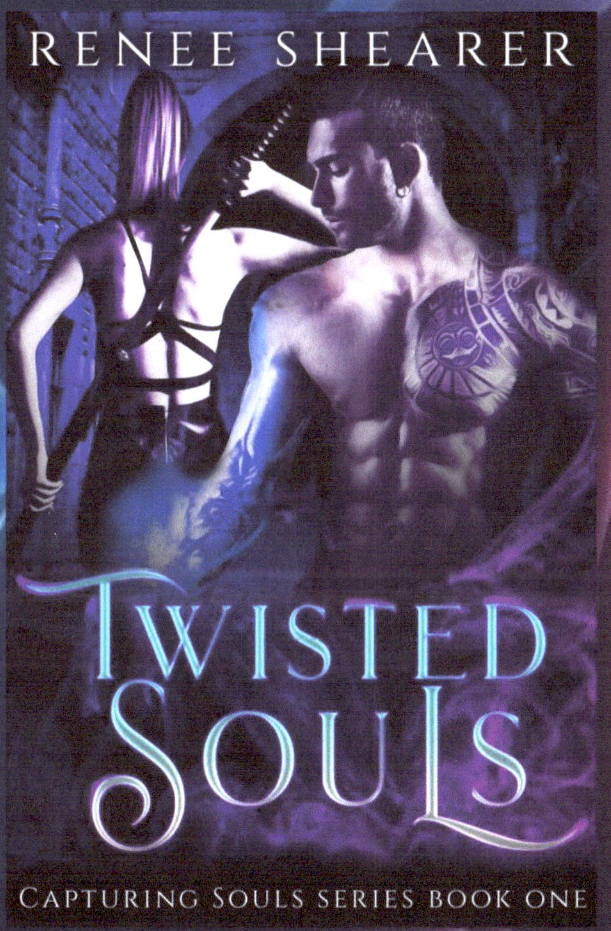

EXCERPT FROM TWISTED SOULS:

The man bowed formally to her, which she found both charming and weird. "Your secret is safe with me."

"Cool. Thanks. Listen I gotta run. I...uh... have a thing, I need to go do. A very important thing"

"A thing? Really JJ, that's the best you can come up with?"

Flashing a grin at the stranger, she silently waved her hands in a swirling pattern. Ignoring Dakota.

"What are you doing?" She could hear the suspicion lacing Dakota's voice.

"Don't worry about it, D." Jess smiled sweetly at Dakota, as she finished with her hands.

Dakota frowned and opened his mouth to reply, "Ribbet!" His eyes widened as he looked at Jess.

"Ribbet, Ribbet, Ribbet!!" every time he tried to talk he would get more frustrated and yelled louder. Soon he was shaking his finger in her face, "Ribbet, Ribbet, Riiiiiiibbbbeeeetttt!"

Jess smirked at the handsome stranger, "See, no violence. I forgot how much fun the subtle shit could be. Gotta jet! Have a good night." She wiggled her fingers and walked away from the two men with an extra sway in her hips.

Meet Carrigan Richards

I&S: Being a new author to our readers, tell us a few random facts about yourself.

I'm seeking my Master's degree in professional writing. I've written and published 6 novels and 1 novella. I used to work at the zoo, and my favorite musician is Tori Amos.

I&S: January Dreams sounds like a really great read! What inspired you to write this story?

I'm not exactly sure how the idea came to me, but I kept imagining two people who shared dreams. Dreams have always been a fascination to me. How real they feel, and how they make you feel when you wake up. It's truly another world concocted by your memories, feelings, worries, experiences, etc. I've always wondered if people can share dreams and not know it. Like if I'm dreaming about someone, do they dream about me? Are my deceased loved ones really visiting me in my dreams?

I&S: Tell our readers about the plot and the characters.

Megan begins having dreams about Casper, a boy from her school whom she hates. But in the dreams they're in love. As she tries to ignore the realness of them, she starts dating brooding and handsome Vincent. She quickly falls in love, even after she realizes they're sharing visions of each other from another life.

Excerpt from January Dreams

Once I see Casper, I'm sure I will calm down. It's the strangest thing. I feel like the dream really happened which is why I have to see him.

I get to school rather impatiently and meet Cherry at my locker. She's talking, but I only half-listen because my eyes are peeled on the vast group of people walking down the hall. I chew the inside of my cheek. I fidget with the strap on my backpack. My eyes dart back and forth looking at every single face that passes by. None of them is Casper.

"Okay, seriously, Megan, what is with you?" Cherry asks.

"Nothing," I mumble.

"Well, could you pay attention to me for five seconds?"

When I don't respond, she lets out an exasperated sigh. "Who are you looking for?"

I don't see him at all. Something is wrong. My heart drops to the pit of my stomach, swirling around with all of the other uneasy feelings.

"Hey," she shouts and grabs my arm, making me look at her. "Calm down. Lay off the Red Bull.

Yeesh. What's the matter with you?"

I can't calm down. She doesn't understand my urgency, but it doesn't matter now. "I have to go check on him."

"Who?"

I swallow. "Casper."

Her eyebrows push together with disbelief in her eyes. "What?"

"He was shot, Cherry. I have to see if he's okay."

"What?" Her eyes enlarge.

"It was a dream," I tell her. "You don't understand." I quickly add as she gives me a disapproving look.

"Meg, it was a dream. It wasn't real. Why does he concern you all of a sudden?"

"I don't know. I gotta go."

She grabs my arm again and the bell rings. "Are you crazy? You can't go to his house."

"I need your phone."

"What?"

"Give me your phone."

When she hands it to me, I google Casper's dad's name and am able to find their address. I'm familiar with the area since it's around my work.

"I have to. Cherry, please. Let me go."

"What's gotten into you?" she shouts as the halls clears.

Currently working on the sequel to January Dreams.

Getting to create different characters and worlds!

BETWEEN EARTH AND EDEN

THE GUARDIAN SERIES

E.L. IRWIN

BETWEEN HEAVEN AND HELL

THE GUARDIAN SERIES

E.L. IRWIN

SUPERNATURAL WORLD OF E. L. IRWIN

I&S: *Supernatural romances are always packed with something unreal. What about your stories - what special features have you added to make them outstanding?*

As far as something unreal goes, I don't know...I guess it depends on whether or not you believe in beings such as angels and demons. I personally do -- I've had encounters with them. In The Guardian Series, I've tried to remain true to how the Bible describes demons and angels. I wanted the reader's encounter with the demons, or hunters as they're called in these books, to make their hair stand on end. I definitely wanted that sense of "other" that should come from an encounter with a supernatural being. I also tried to weave in bits of Celtic and Norse mythology. The character names I chose for this series also have meaning. I include, at the end of book 2, a pronunciation guide and meanings for all the names.

I&S: Tell us more about your latest releases - Between Earth & Eden and Between Heaven & Hell.

Between Earth and Eden is book one in The Guardian Series and it released on October 20th, 2020 to rave reviews. In this book you'll meet all the main characters and get a feel for the plot. There's a bit of a love-triangle as well as some seriously twisted scenes -- sorry, not sorry.

Between Heaven and Hell is book two and it released on November 10th, 2020, also to rave reviews. BHAH concludes this part of the series, however, I am working on more to continue it. In fact, the next book will be called, Between Blood and Stone. BHAH picks up where BEAE left off -- which was on a bit of a cliffhanger. In this novel you travel to another world/realm and meet many fascinating new characters and discover new twists to the plot.

As I mentioned previously, I've had encounters with supernatural beings. As a child, they visited me and I still CLEARLY remember the fear from those visits. I use one of those, the first one, as a scene in the books. As for the rest...like many of my other books, it was the chemistry between characters, and their internal monologues that fueled this story. It was the way both the demon and the angel viewed their human and what their desires for the human were.

I&S: Introduce us to the characters of both stories. Do you have a favorite character? What do you like him/her for?

Both BEAE and BHAH center around the human, Jane, and her twin brother Cash. The twins were in an accident in their youth, leaving Cash in a coma... Now Jane sees and hears things. You'll also meet Theron, Jane's tall, dark and attractive neighbor -- her mysterious neighbor. And then you'll meet Aurek, a customer to the bookstore Jane works at. You'll also see flashes of both the Guardian and the Hunter and their feelings towards Jane.

Good gravy...a favorite character? Mmm, it's hard to pick a favorite. I love them all. Each has their own special quirks and traits that I adore. Theron, I will say, is getting his own story later on, his backstory. That one will be entitled, Between Faith and Fury.

THIS IS A SCENE FROM BEAE:

Theron stepped closer to me... He leaned down, his obsidian eyes nearly on the same level as mine, and said, "Have some patience, love. You'll get to know me in time. When I'm ready. I guarantee it."

I&S: Are you going to add more stories to the stories? What are they going to be about?

Yes, I will be adding more books to the series. One will be about a girl who has a strong affinity for nature, who ends up traveling to Ireland, where she meets some very interesting characters, while getting caught up in a plot to destroy her. This is the one entitled, Between Blood and Stone. Another one I'm plotting out will be Theron's backstory, where you'll get to see just what makes Theron, Theron. That one is entitled, Between Faith and Fury.

I&S: What writing plans do you have for the rest of 2021? When shall we expect a new release from you?

My 2021 goals are to get Between Blood and Stone written, at least the first draft. I'm also working on a sequel to my first book, Out of the Blue. And, I just signed with KISS -- Read & Write Romance (Best Fiction Stories on the Go) so I'll be working with them to publish serialized versions of my books as well as audio versions.

"A Heart-gripping Story With a Fresh Start, Whirlwind of Emotions, Lurking Shadows, Secrets-Lies-Betrayals, True Love and a Sacrifice (Hellish+Teary Cliffhanger!).Fantasy is my beloved genre, & this book blew me away. This story was so different from the books I've read, in a Good way!All Characters were Relatable+Lovable. Except the bad guys, I hated them with a passion!" – Romance Book Lovers' Haven, Goodreads Review, BEAE, 5-STAR *

REVIEWS BY CARINE VERBEKE

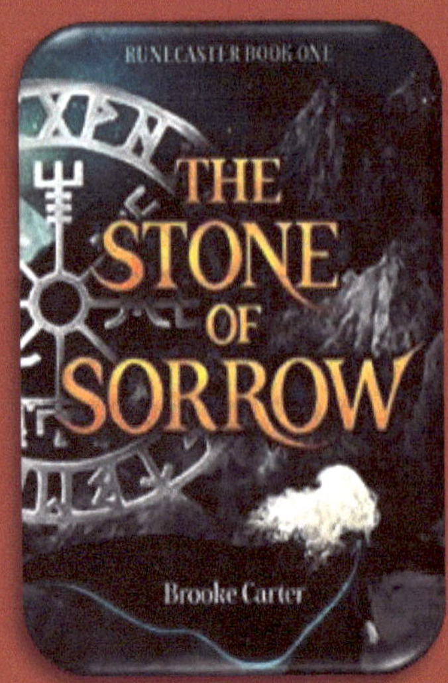

The Stone of Sorrow by Brooke Carter
Book one of Runecaster series
Publisher: Orca Book Publishers

Runa is an interesting character; she has absolutely no self-confidence, neither in her looks nor in her abilities with the runes. Yet, her destiny is all mapped out.

I loved Oski, I loved his humor, his frankness and his murderous side worthy of a valkyrie.

I have to admit that I'm a little afraid of what will happen in the next book because the end gives clues that intrigue me.

Two Witches and a Whiskey by Annette Marie
Book three in The Guild Codex Spellbound
Publisher: Dark Owl Fantasy Inc

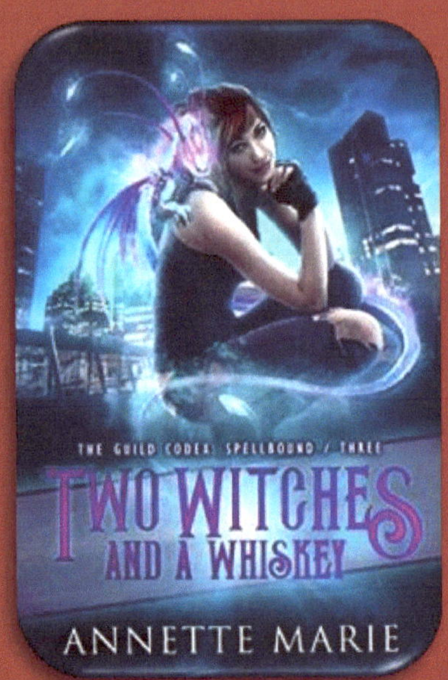

I loved meeting Zac again and I really liked the interactions between Tori and Zac. They have such a different character, yet we can feel that Zac is starting to get attached to the little human.

I liked finding out a little bit more about Kai, I might as well tell you that I didn't suspect what I learned.

Another captivating tome that promises nothing but good things to come!

Taming Demons for Beginners by Annette Marie
Demon Magic and a Martini by Annette Marie
Book one in The Guild Codex : Demonized series
Book five in The Guild Codex Universe
Publisher: Dark Owl Fantasy Inc

I like Robin a lot, probably because she is a bookworm rather than a fighter. Despite the fact that she's afraid of Zylas, she's still attracted to him and she's discovering a lot more about demons.

I made another great discovery with this tome and I feel that Tori and her mages may soon need the help of Robin and Zylas.

A beautiful discovery in a world that I still love so much.

Slaying Monsters for the Feeble by Annette Marie
Book two in The Guild Codex Demonized
Book Seven in The Guild Codex Universe
Publisher: Dark Owl Fantasy Inc

We dive a little deeper into the relationship between Robin and Zylas, we also discover more about what demons are capable of doing.

I'm really looking forward to reading the rest of this series and seeing how Tori's story and Robin's story can come together.

Leo by Diana Nixon
Book Two in Bachelors on Sale series
Publisher: Self Published

I loved seeing the two main characters interacting, sniping at each other all day long, charming each other, laughing and getting to know and respect each other.
I loved this book, I laughed, I cried, I wanted to be in Olivia's shoes and sometimes I wanted to slap her and Leo for being so stubborn and impossible with each other.

An absolutely successful romance to read urgently!

The Alchemist and an Amaretto
by AnnetteMarie
Book five in The Guild Codex Spellbound
Book Six in The Guild Codex Universe
Publisher: Dark Owl Fantasy Inc

Ezra is so touching in this book; I'm under his charm since the beginning of the series but we see him a little more here and we meet Etterran as well.
I liked the rapprochement between Ezra and Tori, the friendship between Aaron, Kai and Ezra which intensifies. We go even more into the story and I can't wait to read more.

Hunting Fiends for the Ill-Equipped by Annette Marie
Book three in The Guild Codex Demonized
Book Nine in The Guild Codex Universe
Publisher: Dark Owl Fantasy Inc

Robin learns a little more about her ancestors, she discovers certain things that disturb her.
She is also attracted to Zylas and it is very touching to see them together.
Zylas is really the character I like; he's a demon so he acts like one, but he still tries to understand Robin and he gets attached to her.

The end is near, the secrets come out, and the stories intertwine.

Lost Talismans and a Tequila by Annette Marie
Book seven in The Guild Codex Spellbound
Book ten in The Guild Codex Universe
Publisher: Dark Owl Fantasy Inc

I really enjoyed the passages with Ezra, Robin and Zylas. It's not a perfect friendship yet but at least they help each other and that's important.

Annette Marie managed to get me to read more than ten books from the same series in less than a month and it'd been a really long time since that happened. So I think it speaks for itself!

Druid Vices and a Vodka by Annette Marie
Book Six in The Guild Codex Spellbound
Book Eight in The Guild Codex Universe
Publisher: Dark Owl Fantasy Inc

The fact that Tori doesn't hesitate for a moment to go and save Zak is an exceptional proof of friendship. I already knew that their relationship was important, but now it's even more so. I still have to admit that my little heart was broken.

This book is intense, a lot of things are happening and you feel like you're getting closer to the end of the story, the answers are coming slowly but they're there.

Warping Minds and other Misdemeanors by Annette Marie & Rob Jacobsen
Book one in The Guild Codex Warped
Book Eleventh in The Guild Codex Universe
Publisher: Dark Owl Fantasy Inc

I like Kit; he's funny and touching, he just had bad luck but that's about to change. Lienna is a very gifted agent. I hope we'll find out more about her in the next volumes. Warping Minds is a success; a good book that puts us in the mood and prepares us for the next ones.

Delivering Evil for Experts by Annette Marie
Book four in The Guild Codex Demonized
Book Thirteenth in The Guild Codex Universe
Publisher: Dark Owl Fantasy Inc

I loved to see the evolution of Robin and Zylas. This last book brings us to the ending we've been hoping for, and most of all, answers our questions. We learn more about the world of demons and personally, I loved it.

An absolutely perfect story to end the series.

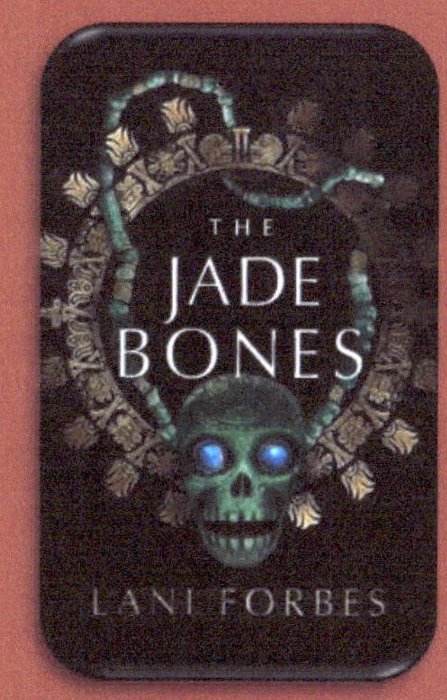

The Jade Bones by Lani Forbes
Book two in The Age of the Seventh Sun trilogy
Publisher: Blackstone Publishing

I enjoyed the duality of Mayana & Ahkin; they are different but complement each other so well.

I find Yemania very touching, she is an absolutely charming young girl who will succeed in questioning her convictions thanks to Ochix. I love him very much. You will get to know him and you will love him too. He is funny, protective, and adorable. Once again, I loved immersing myself in this mythology and I can't wait to read the last volume of the trilogy.

My Italian Valentine by Diana Nixon
Standalone
Publisher: Self Published

What I love about this book is that Angelo is not like other male characters in romance stories in general. That is, he's not arrogant or possessive and he respects Bella and her choices and desires. Another thing I like is that throughout the book we expect a break-up, an event that will destroy their relationship but it never happens. I like to be surprised like that.

I enjoyed the fusion between the two characters. It's a story that reads very quickly and Diana made my heart beat a little faster again.

A Deal with the Elf King by Elise Kova
Book one to Married to Magic series
Publisher: Silver Wing Press
Publication date: November 6th 2020

This was a perfect fantasy romance with Elf; I loved both main characters. Luella and Eldas are really amazing, their relationship is growing and it's a beautiful story. I like Elise Kova's writing style. This story is a must read.

The Gilded Ones by Namina Forna
Book one in Deathless series
Publisher: Delacorte
Publication date: February 9th, 2021

I love this book so much; what happens to Deka is awful, everyone hates her because of her blood but in the end, she becames a strong woman who can defends herself. The story is really good and I can't wait to read the next one.

UNFORGIVEN

USA TODAY AND INTERNATIONAL BESTSELLING AUTHOR

DIANA NIXON

A NEW BREATHTAKING STORY FROM THE USA TODAY & INTERNATIONAL BESTSELLING AUTHOR DIANA NIXON.

Santiago Alcantar killed my parents.
Now it's my turn to take away what he loves most of all…

Losing my parents changed my life forever. I had to learn how to be a fighter. I fought for everything I wanted to have. But when I thought there was nothing I couldn't get, I met her… Gabriela Alcantar. The favorite daughter of my worst enemy.
She made the sorrows of my past return.
I felt weak and helpless again.
I hated it.
As well as I hated her and her entire family.
Because they were the killers. And they could never be forgiven.
Unless… I could make them pay for what they did to me.

"I lied to her… I told her I would never fall in love with her. Then again, I lied to myself. Because my heart already belonged to her…"

A PERFECT NEXT READ FOR THE FANS OF COLLEEN HOOVER, JAMIE MCGUIRE, ANNA TODD & TARRYN FISHER.

GRAB YOUR COPY TODAY!
PRE-ORDER FOR $0.99!

COMING MAY 18T

www.ingramcontent.com/pod-product-compliance
Lightning Source LLC
Chambersburg PA
CBHW042124110726
48006CB00003B/750